Dear Alex,

Thank you very much for the arrangements made at the Nime zero for my visit.

Sincerely yours,

Martin Knirsch

CÉSAR RITZ

ADALBERT CHASTONAY

CÉSAR RITZ

LIFE AND WORK

PUBLISHER:
CÉSAR RITZ FOUNDATION
NIEDERWALD &
HOTELCONSULT "CÉSAR RITZ"
COLLEGES, BRIG

DISTRIBUTION:
"CÉSAR RITZ" COLLEGES

Photos: Norma, Paris; Swiss National Tourist Office, Zurich;
                   Stadtmuseum, Baden-Baden; Hotel Ritz, Paris; Hotel National,
                   Lucerne; Hotel Rigi-Kulm; Walliser Bote, Brig;
                   Mengis Druck und Verlag AG, Visp; Hotel Savoy, London;
                   Hotel Ritz, Paris
Production: Mengis Druck und Verlag AG, Visp, 2005
Distribution: "César Ritz" Colleges, 1897 Le Bouveret, Switzerland

ISBN 3-907816-60-9

Foreword

The extraordinary career of the hotelier César Ritz has been described in a number of publications of which two are of particular importance. The first, written by his wife Marie-Louise Ritz, is entitled "César Ritz" and concentrates primarily on the countless guests, friends, and acquaintances of the Ritz Hotels and their creator.

The second biography – "César Ritz – A Life for the Guest" – is the work of Dr. Werner Kämpfen, former director of the Swiss National Tourist Office in Zurich. He introduces us to the hotelier César Ritz, who planned, organised and revolutionised, who was full of original and bold ideas, and who became a pioneer of the hotel business.

This short biography, which Adalbert Chastonay wrote seventy-five years after the death of César Ritz, is intended for a readership which is little informed about César Ritz, although he was without doubt one of the most important Swiss of the last century. Many thanks to the author.

As the last member of the César Ritz family to have held the position of president and delegate of the "Hotel Ritz" in Paris, I take pleasure in publishing this biography and in presenting the fountain designed by the sculptor Hans Loretan to the parish and inhabitants of Niederwald in lasting remembrance of César Ritz. This fulfils the wish of Marie-Louise Ritz, wife of César Ritz, and my deceased husband Charles, both of whom maintained links with the village of Niederwald throughout their lives.

Geneva, June 30th 1994   Monique Ritz

CONTENTS

The house in Niederwald where César Ritz was born.

ORIGINS

César Ritz, who at the end of the last century was called "The Hotelier of Kings" and "The King of Hoteliers", was born in Niederwald on February 23rd 1850. The small mountain farming hamlet is situated in the high-lying Goms valley in Canton Valais, less than an hour by car from the source of the Rhone River, which links César Ritz's home and his later home of adoption. In Ritz's youth, Niederwald had a population of just over one hundred inhabitants; thus it was – and indeed still is – a very small community.

César was the thirteenth and youngest child of Johann-Anton Ritz and Kreszentia, *née* Heinen. The family lived in simple but well-ordered economic circumstances on the income provided by the mountain farm. The maintenance and upbringing of so many children could not have been an easy task for their parents. Father Ritz held the office of chairman of the parish council for a number of years, and accordingly enjoyed the trust of his fellow citizens.

*Niederwald, César Ritz's native village
in the lower Goms. When he was born in 1850,
it had a population of just 123 inhabitants.*

Youth, Apprenticeship, and Travel Years

The young César Ritz attended primary school in the mountain village of his birth and quickly learned the rudimentary elements of reading, writing, and arithmetic, and perhaps the names of a few important men from Valais and Switzerland. Like most children of his age, he looked after goats, sheep, and cattle in the meadows and alpine pastures of Niederwald during the long school holidays. It was the kind of childhood that people from Valais who later achieved high office and honour liked – and like – to highlight in their biographies. In his parents' house, César learned that life for most people consisted primarily of toil, discipline, and moderation, a hard truth which he was later to experience at different times throughout his own life. It is worth mentioning that the Ritz clan – long-resident, well-known and respected in the Goms valley – produced, before and after César, talented and sought-after wood carvers, altar makers and painters, and also one famous physicist. Perhaps these origins explain why César was so successful in creating and furnishing his hotels, and managing them with so much taste and such a sure feeling for finesse and refinement. Did his parents suspect that César was endowed with such artistic aptitude, and did they entertain hopes that he might one day develop his talents? One thing is certain: the small village in the Valais mountains provided César with a solid foundation for the rest of his life. His parents were aware that it would not be possible for all their children to make a living in Niederwald, and they therefore placed their youngest child with a family in Sion, the cantonal capital, where César learned French and acquired other useful knowledge. Some of the members of the family were ornamental metal workers, and it would not have been surprising if César were to have embarked on a similar profession. In any case, his time in Sion – it lasted about three years – represented a gate to a new world, a gate which was later to open up much wider to him, for it was here that he experienced the desire to meet people from other countries, learn foreign languages, and try to understand foreign

The hotel "Couronnes et Poste" in Brig:
this is where César Ritz's career
started on a "wrong footing".

cultures for the first time. His sojourn in Sion, however, appears not to have borne the fruit in terms of schooling and vocation that his father had hoped, and he subsequently entrusted César to a friend who owned a hotel in Brig for training. There, at the hotel "Couronnes et Poste", César learned the first tricks of the hotel trade as a trainee waiter. Although he was able and willing to learn and a hard worker, his patron did not see him as a potential future hotelier, and the apprenticeship was terminated. But even a recognised master of his trade can make mistakes, as the future was to prove. In 1867, after a brief period as a valet and sexton at Brig Theological College, and in spite of a dire shortage of funds, the seventeen-year-old César travelled to Paris, where the World Exhibition had just opened. It was here that he experienced his first "taste of the big wide world", with which he was later to become fully acquainted. It was his intention to learn hotel management thoroughly. What drove him to this decision? Was it just the wish to be independent of the parental home, to stop living at his parents' expense, or did he want to prove that he was now capable of becoming somebody through his own efforts? Did the intelligent young man perhaps even have an idea of the possibilities that the hotel business could offer to his native Valais, which is blessed with a wealth of beautiful scenery? In any case, the seventeen-year-old boy displayed impressive courage and self-reliance which deserve respect and even admiration.

At a modest inn called the "Hôtel de la Fidélité", César prepared to learn the occupation of waiter from the bottom up. He did not have an easy time. His duties included wiping floors, cleaning shoes, and carrying bags. Vocational training as we understand it today did not yet exist. One learned from practical work, and no theory was provided in the form of vocational schools or courses. One had to observe exactly, heed the instructions of superiors, be agile and nimble – and to discover, remember, and try to fulfil the guests' wishes at all times. Even at this early point in his career, people were amazed at

César's remarkable memory. A well-kept appearance was also essential. César was a willing pupil who quickly learned to satisfy the demands made upon him, and he soon became a highly regarded and popular worker. He rose from apprentice to assistant waiter, then to waiter, and finally to the position of head waiter. Even during this hard formative period, he was keenly aware that his life had not really started before he came to Paris. The initially rather shy young man underwent a rapid transformation. Gripped by ambition and continuously driven by the instinct that he was capable of getting on and doing well, César moved from a mediocre restaurant to a good one, then to a better one, then to an even better one, until finally he obtained a position at the famous "Voisin". His start in his new job was, however, less than encouraging. His employer was not in the least impressed by César's previous employment record, and the newcomer had to start from the beginning all over again. He did so willingly, and he was never to regret it: in his own words, the "Voisin" was his real vocational college.

At the "voisin"

Paris was a great metropolis not only because of the World Exhibition, for it was the glittering focus of the political, economic, and cultural life of France and therefore possessed a major intellectual magnetism and appeal. César, who throughout his life regretted not having enjoyed a formal higher education, hungrily absorbed the many new impressions, thus broadening his mind and at the same time gaining the self-confidence and self-assurance which were essential for a young man wanting to make a name for himself in life and seeking success. At the "Voisin" he also learned about the mysteries of the art of cooking, thereby acquiring qualifications indispensable to a hotelier. It was here that he met the master chef Auguste Escoffier who, apart from his mastery of his trade, was endowed with intellectual prowess and a reputation which resulted in excellent contacts with major contemporary figures in the worlds of literature, theatre and, music, for instance Edmond de Goncourt, Marcel Proust, Alexandre Dumas Jr., Théophile Gautier, George Sand, and Sarah Bernhardt. Auguste Escoffier accompanied César through many important phases of his career, was an indispensable employee and advisor, and finally a true friend. César also made a number of other important encounters at this time. At the "Splendide", which in today's terms would count as a five-star hotel, he met guests from the New World, successful businessmen from industry, trade, banking and insurance. Like César, many of them came from humble backgrounds and had attained immense wealth, social standing, and political influence through hard work, daring, and stamina. They were delighted by the young Maître d'hôtel's impeccable appearance, conduct, and service, appreciated his abilities, and had faith in his vocational prospects. César Ritz was in turn impressed by these men of the world, and he may well have conjectured that he, too, might be capable of similar success. He endeavoured to form a detailed impression of these people, to under-

*The famous French chef Auguste Escoffier
(1846–1935), whose creations included
the dessert Pêche Melba, was César Ritz's
closest associate and confidant.*

stand their wishes and tastes in terms of food, wine, music, and pleasure, and sought to satisfy all their needs as guests.

Sojourn in Vienna

Work and change suited César Ritz totally. 1873 took him to Vienna, where another World Exhibition had just been opened, and where he worked in the renowned French restaurant "Les Trois Frères Provençaux". Vienna was then the city of the Imperial and Royal Monarchy of Austro-Hungary, a different world, a different culture and mentality, albeit temporarily under the influence of the euphoria of victory in the Franco-Prussian war under which France in particular had suffered and of which Ritz was long to harbour unpleasant memories. Although himself of Alemannic stock, César tended more towards the French and English ways of life, with which he was also better acquainted through his knowledge of the languages, than the emphatically Germanic style which was prevalent in Vienna at the time. In spite of his heavy workload, he was not unreceptive to the charms of this city on the beautiful blue Danube, and he also found time to fall in love with a charming young Viennese girl. Perhaps it was his memories of Vienna which prompted him, over twenty years later, to engage the Waltz King, Johann Strauss Junior, as a musical entertainer at the hotel "Savoy" in London at a truly princely fee. It was in the city on the Danube that he decided to widen his experience of the so-called seasonal hotel trade. Owing to their mild winters, the French and Italian Rivieras had opened up a new and interesting area of work, and César Ritz took up managerial positions in various important hotels, such as the "Grand-Hôtel" in Nice.

A SWIFT DECISION AND AN IMPORTANT ENCOUNTER

Actively encouraged by his fellow Swiss countryman Weber, Ritz followed his interval on the Riviera by taking up the position of restaurant director at the hotel "Rigi-Kulm" in Canton Lucerne. Even then, Mount Rigi was popular for its outstanding views and was particularly famous for its incomparable sunrises. People flocked there from all over the world, especially from England, France, and Germany, but also from further afield, to experience this magnificent natural spectacle, sometimes even walking up on foot or riding on the backs of mules. Here Ritz gave a particularly impressive demonstration of his inventiveness and decisiveness and his talent for assessing and mastering difficult situations rapidly. The following event proved to be of crucial importance in his career.

On one of the often still light and warm September days, the weather on the Rigi mountain suddenly changed. The temperature fell to minus eight degrees and a gale-force wind sprang up. To complete the disaster, the heating in the hotel failed. On top of it all, a Thomas Cook party of some forty demanding Americans was on its way to the Rigi, where they were expected for lunch. Hotel director Weber wrung his hands in desperation, but César Ritz leaped into action. The table d'hôte was moved into a small dining room which was quickly made ready. The ornamental palms were lifted out of their massive copper pots and the pots were converted into heaters. Forty hot bricks, packed in woollen cloths, warmed the guests' frozen feet, and the menu was adjusted radically to meet the new circumstances. Everybody was delighted with the improvised solution, and news of the event was soon passed around. Ritz was suddenly known as the master of the difficult situation.

It was at the "Rigi" that he became aware of the importance of public relations in the catering trade. If a restaurant was to become and remain known, it was essential that it become a subject of conversation.

The hotel "Rigi-Kulm", where César Ritz demonstrated his talent for improvisation and organisation for the first time.

Later on, also at the "Rigi Kulm", Ritz met a man who was to be of major importance in his future career: Colonel Alphons Pfyffer von Altishofen, architect and engineer, builder and owner of the hotel "National" in Lucerne, which enjoyed an excellent reputation both in Switzerland and abroad as a real luxury hotel. When Colonel Pfyffer, who had heard about the quick-wittedness and decisiveness of the restaurant director, later called on Ritz to offer him the job of manager of his hotel, Ritz leaped at the opportunity, even though his new employer could not offer him particularly good terms since the hotel was not doing especially well, in spite of its high standing. But Ritz wanted to get even better acquainted with the big wide world and to become independent as soon as possible. The excellent reputation he had acquired in his previous places of employment soon attracted guests to Lucerne, and the "National" became a meeting place for the European intellectual, influential, and financial elite. Representatives of the European and American business worlds also came to stay, and they returned time and time again. Under its new director, the hotel "National" became the scene of glittering parties which Ritz, commissioned by the very wealthy, organised with the greatest success.

Colonel Pfyffer, his two sons, and Ritz remained in contact over a period of many years. The simple mountain farm boy, who still suffered from the gaps in his formal education, found an excellent mentor and competent advisor in the open-minded and cultivated Lucerne hotelier, especially regarding financial matters, which at that time were uncharted waters for Ritz.

The hotel "National" was open only during the summer months and was therefore not able to satisfy Ritz's career plans and material needs. He spent the rest of the year back on the Riviera, where he worked in succession as director of restaurants and hotels in highly respected establishments in Nice, Menton, Cannes, and to the northwest in Biarritz. Thanks to Ritz, fruitful collaboration sprang up between the hotels he managed and the "National" in Lucerne. His guests knew that where Ritz wielded the sceptre, luxury, comfort, and elegance were ensured. During these years he also tried his hand as lessee of the hotel "Roches Noires", not far from La Trouville, an experiment which turned out a financial failure and led to his return to the "National" in Lucerne, which in all truth he had left somewhat prematurely.

The hotel "National" in Lucerne, today.

Between Monte Carlo and Lucerne

For eight years Ritz managed both the "Grand-Hôtel" in Monte Carlo and the "National" in Lucerne. In Monte Carlo his guests included the Prince of Wales, the English heir to the throne, who arrived with an impressive entourage. The prince was impressed by what Ritz and his "Grand-Hôtel" had to offer, and this triggered a regular stream of other distinguished guests who reinforced and propagated the excellent reputation of this first-class hotel and its director.

Hotels are rarely a permanent home. Most frequently, they are just a place of temporary sojourn, a brief abode between two travel destinations, a meeting place to conduct business, a studio perhaps for artists, a place to enjoy oneself, and possibly a place of refuge for a lonely person. Thus the hotel trade has many different sides and is a profession with a high degree of responsibility. Often, the demands made on a hotelier go beyond the mere satisfaction of material needs and he becomes a kind of confidant with whom guests can discuss quite personal matters. Ritz took this aspect of his vocation seriously and exercised absolute discretion. He himself thought of it in these terms: "See all and yet have seen nothing; hear all and forget having heard it; know more than others, and keep quiet about it."

Between Monte Carlo and Lucerne, Ritz grew into the role of an independent hotelier, a profession which requires great sensitivity for the psychology of the guest. The hotelier must foresee future needs and developments in his trade and be prepared to adapt. A certain creative talent and inventiveness are essential. Ritz was now well prepared for these tasks; his own hotel could now become reality.

Hotel "Minerva" in Baden-Baden:
César Ritz's first own hotel.

BADEN-BADEN

In 1888, Ritz was able to acquire the hotel and restaurant "de la Conversation" in Baden-Baden. He was given priority over no less than fifty applicants, for the man from the Rigi, Lucerne, and Monte Carlo had already achieved a degree of recognition which triggered confidence and nurtured expectation of further success. The purchase went through, thanks largely to the financial support of Otto Kahn, an influential figure in local business.

Baden-Baden was already a heavily visited spa. The members of high society who could afford regular holidays, travel, and leisure liked to spend their winters on the coast and their summers in the mountains, while the periods in-between offered the opportunity to pay a visit to a spa, which was conducive to good health.

The risk that Baden-Baden represented – for that it undoubtedly was – turned into a success. The German Emperor, kings, princesses and princes, politicians, and high ranking military officers stopped off on a regular basis at Ritz's hotel and spread his name abroad. He became better acquainted with Germany, and the Germans became better acquainted with him, and because they valued thoroughness and a strict, intelligent style of leadership, he soon became their man. The excellent upswing in his business also made it possible for him to acquire the local hotel "Minerva".

Both businesses proved to be major successes and were very soon making vast profits. Ritz was well aware of the value of money and was thoroughly prepared to invest in his enterprises. Naturally, he was keen on making money with his profession, but it must be said to his credit that this was not the only reason that he became a hotelier. He appears to have shunned neither hard work nor financial cost in the interests of his projects, and all the other hotels in Baden-Baden also benefited from his untiring activity and inventiveness. Nevertheless, some of his peers in the business grudged him his enormous success, to the extent that he was urgently advised by one of his friends not to go out alone at night. Competition is seldom tolerated very well, although it is really the engine of all economic progress.

The success of the enterprise in Baden-Baden prompted Otto Kahn to help with the acquisition of the "Hôtel de Provence" in Cannes, an establishment to which Ritz had a strong personal attachment.

THE STEP
TO ENGLAND

Thanks to his guests in Lucerne, Monte Carlo, Baden-Baden, and the other places where he had been active in the hotel trade, the excellent reputation enjoyed by the hotelier Ritz spread to England, and especially to London.

London towards the end of the 19th century was a powerful and fascinating focus of international business life. From all over the world – from the continent and overseas – business, money, and political influence flooded into the metropolis, and their presence had a lasting effect on the prosperity of science, art, and especially the theatre and music. English society began to change.

At regular intervals, financially strong backers tried to persuade Ritz to buy or build a luxury hotel in London. He was not, however, at all keen on these proposals, for the circumstances in England at the time were not particularly favourable to the realisation of such a project. These included strict observance of legislation regarding Sunday closing, early closing of pubs in the evening, high prices for wine, costly licence fees, tough competition between hotels and restaurants, and the English clubs, which were sacred to the male component of the upper classes. The would-be backers envisaged a hotel of first-rate standards geared to attract a select international clientele, and the rapid improvement in transportation links appeared to favour such a project. After much hesitation, Ritz let himself be persuaded to take on the semi-official management of the hotel "Savoy", which was being refurbished. At the same time, he wanted to continue running his businesses in Baden-Baden and Cannes. Eventually, Ritz's conditions were – however hesitantly – accepted, in spite of the danger that he would be taking on an excessive workload.

Ritz's first concern was the supervision of the furnishing of the modernised hotel "Savoy" and preparations for its official opening. It had not escaped him that the management of this establishment was full of shortcomings which crystallised into a loss at the end

The menu from the hotel "Savoy" in London,
dated June 25th 1895, with the signatures of famous
guests such as the future Belgian King Albert I.

of the year. He was also aware that his participation was coveted probably only because the board of directors expected him to pass on his enthusiasm for The "Savoy" to his many personal friends and acquaintances, acquired during his previously successful activities; and it seems that on this point he was not far off the mark.

At the "Savoy", Ritz proved to be an experienced and energetic administrator. After just one year, the hotel showed encouraging success, and in the following two to three years its financial position increased by leaps and bounds.

Every major political, business, or social event brought droves of noblemen, politicians, business leaders, and artists to the British capital, where they wanted to experience the already almost legendary reputation of the "Savoy" for themselves. As an organiser, Ritz introduced the boldest of innovations, unconcerned about the cost of their realisation. The results always proved him correct. His enormous success led one English journalist to call Ritz a disciple of Midas, who turned everything he touched into gold. A further contemporary writer remarked: "Thanks to Ritz, England will soon be habitable. He has revolutionised the hotels and the deep-rooted habits of English society, but he will never be successful in changing those legal provisions which constrict and hinder our social life. The law does not show any consideration for persons, especially actors, and nothing in the world could convince the English that it is not an offence against decency and good taste to eat in a public restaurant on Sunday. They are condemned to their cold lamb chops and the monotonous boredom of their Sundays." But this prophet was to be proved wrong. Ritz understood the problem, promised change, made his various contacts with the authorities pull some strings, and triumphed once again.

THE ROMAN YEARS
1891–1895

The idea of establishing the "Grand-Hôtel" in Rome stemmed from influential groups among the Italian aristocracy who knew Ritz from Lucerne. But the shareholders of the hotel company "Savoy" were also very interested in the realisation of such a project. The time appeared to be favourable. Rome, the Eternal City, with its innumerable, matchless works of art, would always draw people. The transatlantic maritime links had significantly improved, and this resulted in a regular stream of guests from overseas. Thus a new joint stock company was quickly founded to supervise the construction project. A suitable plot of land was available, but there was already a building on it which was only semi-completed, owing to financial problems. The intention was to finish, enlarge, and furnish the building as a luxury hotel. Ritz was named director and thus bore full responsibility for the success of the venture. Very soon, however, it became apparent that the construction, organisation, and administration of the new hotel would require his attention to a degree that would force him to reduce his activities in other places, and he thus bade farewell to Baden-Baden, and later – not without regret – to the "Hôtel de Provence" in Cannes.

To Ritz, Rome represented an interesting new sphere of action. The "Grand-Hôtel" was to be a major success. The Eternal City made a deep impression on Ritz and, accompanied by his friend Alphons Pfyffer Junior, he visited the most important works of art, proved almost insatiable in his desire to acquire more knowledge, asked countless questions, and wanted to see and get to know everything.

The opening of the "Grand-Hôtel" was a major event. No less than 1,500 people attended, including representatives from the Quirinal, the Vatican, the government, and the aristocracy. The mayor of Rome, a real-life prince, welcomed Ritz in his speech as the new "Caesar" who had come to conquer Rome.

In order to relieve the burden placed upon her husband, Marie-Louise Ritz assumed responsibility for the furnishing and decoration of the rooms, a very costly and difficult task which she carried out successfully and with great skill.

The opening of the "Grand-Hôtel" was preceded by an event which once again demonstrated Ritz's perception of human nature and diplomatic skills. During the furnishing of the new hotel the 200 locally hired workers went on strike, and nothing could persuade them to recommence work. Ritz travelled to Rome immediately and solved the problem in a flash. He gathered the strikers together, reminded them of the obligations they had entered into, and served them an ample, typically Italian meal, which – washed down with copious Chianti – substantially contributed to the re-establishment of peaceful labour relations. Ritz made sure that the "Grand-Hôtel" was equipped with the most modern furnishings. He paid special attention to the sanitary installations and the lighting, and he was a pioneer in the introduction of indirect lighting, some time before his professional peers.

The "Grand-Hôtel" in Rome soon became a huge success, at first financially, as well as otherwise. Ritz stipulated that Rome was to have a winter season, an idea which soon proved promising. Once again, wealthy guests from hotels which Ritz had previously managed, or in which he had worked as a consultant or had participated financially, followed in his wake. The social life of Rome changed. Wealthy, life-loving people invaded the Roman world of artists, pilgrims, and diplomats in search of amusement. Thanks to the "Grand-Hôtel", Rome became a place of glittering parties with many international guests, in spite of the serious crises which gripped Italy at the time. The Italian government considered that Ritz's activities and initiative were favourable to the course of their affairs, and during the hotel's second season King Umberto acknowledged Ritz's services by making him a knight of the order of the crown. This honour was followed by a private audience with Pope Leo XIII. Ritz counted these two experiences among the most valued memories of his life.

31

THE TRAVELLING HOTELIER AND EXPERT

Between 1890 and 1900, as a recognised expert on the hotel business, Ritz reached the pinnacle of his career. Before 1893, he had been in the habit of travelling primarily between London, Baden-Baden, and Cannes. Thereafter, however, his travels and his stays in these various destinations increased to include London, Aix-les-Bains, Rome, Lucerne; later Frankfurt, Wiesbaden, Monte Carlo, and Biarritz; and then Salsomaggiore and Paris. Ritz was busy with the construction and organisation of a number of famous establishments. There were the "Savoy" and the new "Carlton" in London, both of which demanded his presence at least occasionally, the "Grand-Hôtel" in Rome, the "Frankfurter Hof" in Frankfurt, and the "Grand-Hôtel des Thermes" in Salsomaggiore. He also supervised the operations of the "Grand-Hôtel" in Palermo, the "Ritz" restaurant in Biarritz, the hotels "Claridges", "Hyde-Park" and "Londres" in London, and the "Kaiserhof" and "Augusta-Viktoria" in Wiesbaden. And, of course, the "Grand-Hôtel" in Monte Carlo and the "National" in Lucerne. As co-founder and first president of the "Hotels Ritz Development Company" in London, whose object was the inauguration and operation of luxury hotels, Ritz drafted plans for the construction of similar establishments in Cairo, Madrid, and Johannesburg, and at the same time realised the plan for his own hotel in Paris. Hoteliers from Germany and the United States came to Ritz for advice, and he supervised no less than eight hotels with 2,000 hotel beds in his capacity of hotelier and expert. And although the initiative behind certain hotel establishments and financial interests in existing undertakings can be traced to former guests, without Ritz the projects would probably not have been realised so quickly and the desired standard of quality achieved. His reputation and his authority as an internationally recognised expert were enormous at the time. Who could have predicted this advancement? When, during the Lucerne years, Colonel Pfyffer once expressed regret that there was still no hotel of the class of his "National" in London,

Paris, Rome, or Vienna, Ritz is supposed to have replied that the reason that there were as yet no hotels of this standard in these cities was that they did not have a César Ritz. And, in fact, it was Ritz who was to turn this idea into reality and to fill the gaps.

It seems inevitable that the permanent strain of his work and his many taxing and frequently difficult journeys would sooner or later result in serious health problems. His doctors and his friends did not hide their concern and warned him to be careful and to take adequate rest. Nevertheless, the number and urgency of the tasks continued to dictate his pace of work.

The "Carlton" in London, established under Ritz's direction, proved to be a sensational success, and once again the Prince of Wales was among his very first guests. There were, however, also some set-backs at this time: a scarlet fever epidemic in Salsomaggiore caused the hotel to empty rapidly and resulted in severe financial losses, and to round off the problems a dispute arose with a very rich and self-confident American lady who had been requested to vacate her suite in "The Ritz" in Paris for the English heir to the throne. This lady, whose opinion of blue-blooded royals was apparently not the highest, categorically refused to do as she was told, and Ritz, whose powers of persuasion usually turned out to his advantage, had to accept defeat this time. On this occasion he is reported to have stated the frequently quoted saying: "The guest is always right."

The Place Vendôme in Paris with the hotel "Ritz" on the left.

His own hotel: "The Ritz" in Paris

Even during his most successful period, one of Ritz's main objectives was still to run his own hotel. To build, furnish and manage his establishment entirely according to his own ideas in a carefully selected location had always been his greatest wish. This hotel could, however, only be in Paris, for it was here that he had gained the initial experience and knowledge which had fitted him to hold especially demanding posts later on. Ritz wanted his hotel to set an unprecedented example in terms of comfort and elegance. Had he followed the suggestions of some of his advisors, he might have built something in the nature of the mammoth colossi which were the trend at the time. Instead, "The Ritz" in Paris was a medium-sized establishment dedicated to comfort, luxury, and hygiene, and above all to hospitality. In other words, it offered an ambience in which the visitor was not just a profitable customer but a real guest, and the hotelier a host in the best sense of the word. The personal element was important in this establishment. That is how Ritz wanted it, and so it came about.

The construction of the hotel, which, with some 150 rooms was still of considerable size, went through seemingly without a hitch, and Ritz also solved the difficult business of finance almost immediately. In this context, the following anecdote is told: The acquisition of the necessary real estate for the hotel "Ritz" on the Place de Vendôme, already a work of art in its own right, required a swift decision. Ritz made this decision without hesitation and without discussing it in advance with the other members of his company. Some years previously he had given the vineyard owner Marnier, a physically small but very ambitious man, an excellent tip to create the brand name "Le Grand Marnier" for his product. As a token of thanks, Marnier advanced him the money for the land. The board of directors of the Ritz Company were first surprised, then nonplussed, and finally very pleased, for all that was left to do was to pay off the credit. It is interesting to note that the funds for the hotel "Ritz" came primarily from

*The entrance of the hotel "Ritz" in Paris
decked out for Christmas.*

English sources, very much to the frustration of the French, who had taken a very guarded attitude towards the project. The English, business-minded and passionate travellers, wanted Paris to have a hotel appropriate to their social standing, as it were, a home away from home, and a host whom they knew well and in whose competence they had full confidence.

In the experienced and well-known Charles Mewès, Ritz found an expert who had a flair for combining tradition and modernity. Furthermore, Mewès possessed the necessary critical mind and personal courage not only to appreciate Ritz's wishes and views but also to improve upon them whenever this appeared necessary. Ritz always emphasised that he did not understand anything about construction, aesthetics, and decorative problems. His stated aim was to build a hotel that would represent a paragon in terms of modern hygiene, comfort, and rational management. And indeed, the modest reputation of the leading Paris hotels at the time thoroughly justified this project.

He took special care with the interior design of his hotel, paying particular attention to the proportions and furnishings of the various rooms in order to make them as rational as possible to manage; to the enlargement of the public rooms and the restaurant at the expense of the non-profitable vestibule; to indirect lighting, the equipment of the rooms of all floors with luxurious bathrooms, and to the laying out of appropriate green areas in spite of the limited space. Mewès also proved to be a very competent advisor on the choice of furniture. He recommended genuine period furniture, which brought an understandably defensive reaction from Ritz in view of the costs, and it was finally agreed to install artistically valuable period reproductions. Marie-Louise and César Ritz later admitted that this collaboration with Mewès represented a genuine apprenticeship in fine artistic taste.

César Ritz (1850–1918).

The energy and care that Ritz lavished on the construction and furnishing of "his" hotel was truly impressive, and his work and considerable financial expense were crowned by a huge and well-deserved success. "I want a hotel in which a gentleman would wish to live", said Ritz, and this is exactly what he achieved. The outcome drew the following praise from the owner of the building: "The hotel 'Ritz' is a small establishment about which I can say that I am very proud to know that its name is linked with mine."

In 1898, the cream of society from Paris, Rome, and London arrived for the opening celebration and praised the genius, imaginativeness, and drive of the great César Ritz. Distinguished former guests from other European countries and overseas followed in their footsteps and paid homage to the man who was probably the most successful hotelier of the latter part of the 19th century. The shy young boy from the cramped farmhouse parlour in the isolated Valais mountain village of Niederwald was now truly "The King of Hoteliers".

Illness and death

The life and work of César Ritz are not free of an element of tragedy. In June 1902, at the pinnacle of his success and reputation, he collapsed in the middle of his work. He was in the process of preparing for the reception of the new king of England, Edward VII, when he was notified of the king's sudden illness and impending operation. The festive nature and importance of the occasion had prompted a number of well-known London hotels to enter into competition with the "Carlton" for the honour of staging this reception – which, however, Ritz was determined to win. Because he was faced with so many urgent tasks in his other undertakings at the same time, he probably refused to acknowledge the first warning signs of serious fatigue. When the news of the king's illness reached him, he collapsed and fell unconscious in his office, exhausted both physically and mentally. It was the beginning of a emotional disorder which was to drag on for over sixteen years and condemn him to almost complete passivity. Initially, the medical prognosis was rather vague. His circle of family and friends were fairly confident that his state of exhaustion could be overcome with time, complete rest, competent medical attention, diversion, and possibly stays at a health resort and travel. The international press seized on Ritz's sudden illness, thus proving his degree of fame, and the family felt obliged to disseminate calming news. Hopes were further raised by Ritz's resilient constitution and strong will, although at the time medical science was still faced with a largely unresearched field in the treatment of the depressive neurosis from which he was suffering. At times, his state of health really did improve; his former zest and capacity for enthusiasm appeared to revive, and Ritz started to work again and play an active role in business. It was not long, however, before he suffered a relapse which was to last for a considerable time. There were times when his doctors and friends believed that a return to his familiar work would be an effective means of restoring his health, and the attempt was risked on their advice. After a prolonged journey to Egypt, where he was present at the laying of the foundation stone of the hotel "Ritz" in Cairo, he threw himself once more into business life. His temperament was such, however, that he was incapable of moderation in his work, and on July 1st 1903 he suffered a further breakdown which was to prove much more serious. Long periods in a semi-comatose state were interspersed by occasional rays of hope when memories of the times of his success penetrated the veil, and he even had one or two exciting new ideas which were subsequently realised in the "Ritz" in Paris, among them a particularly rational design for a connecting corridor between the hotel and an added annex. Later, this connecting corridor served the finest shops in Paris for advertising purposes and proved very profitable financially. But Ritz's will to live and his vitality were broken, and in 1906 he was moved to a mental hospital in Lausanne. Practical experience in the healing and alleviation of this serious illness was still in its infancy, and the family lived in constant conflict between hope and despair. Some time later, Ritz was moved to the "Eichmatt" near Küssnacht in Canton Schwyz, and a slight and unfortunately only temporary improvement in his state of health allowed him to travel once again from Lucerne over the Grimsel pass to Valais and visit his home in Niederwald. He cherished great plans for his native village, including clean streets, healthy water, and electric light. He wanted to make it possible for industrious young men to learn a craft and afterwards to see and experience the big wide world. Later, Ritz's descendants took up this idea and realised it through the establishment of the "César Ritz Foundation". Soon afterward his visit to Niederwald, Ritz entered an institution in Küssnacht for medical attention and care where, on October 23rd 1918, he died alone because his wife was unable to reach him in time, owing to problems in crossing the frontier. César Ritz was granted but sixty-eight years of life, sixteen of which he was obliged to spend in professional inactivity, a truly terrible fate for this active man who in his best days had enjoyed such great and international renown.

A BRIEF TRIBUTE

César Ritz, who was named by his admiring contemporaries "The Hotelier of Kings and The King of Hoteliers", earned these names partly owing to his relations over many years with the crowned heads of Europe, in particular with the English royal family, whose heir to the throne and later king Edward VII was a regular guest at his hotels. Above all, however, the distinction was justified by the high quality of the services that Ritz rendered at all times in the hotels he managed, established, or advised.

Anyone who aspires to lasting success in the hotel business must master his profession to the point of perfection. He must be outgoing and at the same time diplomatic, have a good knowledge of human nature, speak a number of foreign languages, and be capable of foreseeing, adjusting to, and preparing for possible later developments in his trade. He must be a good organiser, an excellent manager of personnel, and able to weather the unavoidable set-backs from which even the hardest-working person is not spared in this occupation. Moreover, he should be practically inclined and knowledgeable about the rational administration of a hotel. Above all, he must love his profession more than anything else.

Ritz possessed these attributes and was thus well equipped for the career of a particularly successful hotelier. Starting at the bottom, he acquired the necessary skills through hard and sustained work. He was intelligent, eager to learn, decisive; he grasped new and sometimes difficult situations quickly and usually knew the right course of action. Proof of these qualities is furnished by the important decisions he made throughout his career, not only at the hotel "Rigi-Kulm", but also in difficult situations in Lugano, Lucerne, Monaco, Monte Carlo, Rome, Salsomaggiore, and elsewhere.

The age he lived in – it was a time of undreamed-of economic growth and rapid technological development – was favourable to his career since it called for the construction of new hotels, and especially for luxury hotels. A wealthy new society, whose rhythm of life was exhilarated by a booming economy, set the highest store on living, eating, drinking, and pleasure, and luxury hotels had to satisfy these demands under all circumstances. The world had grown larger and wider and, thanks to the development of transport and communications, much more accessible. Ritz recognised at an early stage the undreamed-of possibilities offered to a determined person schooled by practical work. Over the course of the years, he rose to become an internationally recognised hotel business expert and was greatly sought after as an advisor on both sides of the Atlantic.

His most remarkable achievement was not the realisation of new luxury hotels, but of a new type of hotel, the hotel "Ritz", embodied and represented above all by "The Ritz" in Paris, but also by the other hotels he founded, co-founded or managed, and advised. Ritz hotels represent the highest class of luxury, designed first and foremost for particularly demanding and discriminating guests. It was considered to be the epitome of good taste to eat, live, and enjoy oneself at Ritz's establishments.

Ritz the hotelier spared no effort to become fully acquainted with each of his guests, to consider their wishes at all times, and to fulfil them promptly. This extraordinary achievement was possible only because of his incredible memory, and it was said that he virtually never forgot a face.

It was not long – at the latest by his interval at the hotel "Rigi-Kulm" – before Ritz recognised the importance of public relations for a flourishing hotel business. He remained more or less in permanent contact with his former guests via letter, telegram, and regular visits, and the visitors' books of the Ritz hotels are particularly impressive.

His careful consideration of the sophisticated demands of his guests constantly prompted Ritz to improve his range of services. This extended to the design and furnishing of the living, sleeping, and recreation rooms, and to the vistas from the windows onto green parks or interesting streets which occasionally afforded a view of a passing royal coach.

Another of Ritz's strong points, and thus of the Ritz hotels, was his personnel. During the best times, there were two employees for every guest, and although this ratio could not be maintained for very long, it nevertheless illustrates Ritz's attentiveness to the customer. At all times, he employed an excellently schooled team of virtually impeccable service staff which enabled him, among other things, to take over the organisation of large and complicated ceremonies and celebrations outside his own domain, to design them to perfection and to run them with unfailing success. Events of this kind included the diamond anniversary of Queen Victoria's reign and the coronation of King Edward VII, to name but two. A particularly outstanding feature was the high quality of the cuisine. Ritz placed the greatest importance on his kitchen staff and was time and time again successful in recruiting master chefs, including the famous Auguste Escoffier, whom we have already mentioned. Another of Ritz's talents was the selection and management of personnel, and he spared no expense on the training and further education of the employees he had so carefully selected. He was particularly good at furthering their resourcefulness and self-confidence, and they rewarded his trust with faultless work, loyalty, and devotion. There are numerous examples of their steadfast commitment. When Ritz, deeply hurt and disappointed because of an intrigue against him, terminated his contract at the "Savoy" overnight, the managing staff decided to follow his example in spite of considerable economic disadvantages.

Was Ritz creative? The only possible answer to this question is an unqualified "yes", without any fear of contradiction.

What Ritz realised with his hotels was not only the satisfaction of long-unsatisfied needs or the mere adaptation to newly arising demands, for he developed his own style of living, dwelling, eating, and enjoying life – a style which influenced fashion and revolutionised deeply-rooted habits as, for example, in England.

Ritz possessed the ability to recognise what high society, and thus future guests, would want and request, not only today, but also tomorrow and the day after. The design and furnishing of "his" hotel "Ritz" in Paris represented the faithful realisation of his ideas. Friends and confidants recognised the confirmation of his creative talents in his work, doubtlessly inherited from the well-known and respected artists of the Ritz lineage from the Valais mountains. His parents' hopes that their youngest child would evidence artistic talent were fulfilled, although in a different field. Ritz created a new kind of hotel and at the same time a hitherto unknown way of living, and a culinary and social culture. Had he not been endowed with creative talents, he could never have achieved what he did in his life's work, which has outlived him and his times.

It is no exaggeration to describe Ritz as a great pioneer of the hotel business whose achievements have ensured his place among the major personalities of the latter part of the 19th century. His immense talent and his outstanding accomplishments often received appropriate recognition during his lifetime from his guests, the authorities, and the press. César Ritz died almost exactly seventy-five years ago, but his name is a byword which will remain as long as there are people who set store on reinforcing their elevated social status by regular stays at a "Ritz" hotel.

César and Marie-Louise Ritz as a newly-wed couple (1888).

Marie-Louise Ritz

The professional and social rise of César Ritz and his international status as a hotelier would have been unthinkable without his wife Marie-Louise Ritz, *née* Beck. She was a native of Alsace and her mother ran a small hotel in Menton. She was seventeen years younger than Ritz, and he married her when he was thirty-eight. In contrast to his usual habit of grasping an opportunity with both hands and striking while the iron was hot, he allowed himself considerable time before he took this step.

The marriage of Marie-Louise and César Ritz was preceded by a long period of comradeship and friendship, a period which they evidently needed to get to know each other better, perhaps as a result of the difference in their ages. According to both partners, it was Marie-Louise who decided on the wedding. By this time they knew each other well enough to embark on a new adventure together, an adventure which proved – with the exception of César's long period of suffering – to be very happy.

Marie-Louise was an ideal spouse for her husband, a true friend and a great source of support on good and bad days, in times of success, and during the long, trying years of illness. Intelligent, cosmopolitan, energetic, endowed with a talent for languages and very familiar with the hotel business, she supported her busy husband in both word and deed. Her culture and her interest in art and literature proved especially beneficial in the fulfilment of her many responsibilities, and she played a decisive and productive role in the highly successful interior decoration and design of the hotels in Rome and Paris.

When his severely impaired state of health no longer permitted Ritz to bear the increasingly large burden of his many professional commitments, Marie-Louise courageously and energetically picked up the reins of management of the most important businesses. Having her own origins in the hotel trade, she had valuable expe-

Marie-Louise Ritz in her apartment at "The Ritz"
in Paris. Until her death in 1961, she was the heart
and soul of the world-famous hotel, and she and her son
Charles established the César Ritz Foundation.

rience in running a business on her own. In addition, she had taken a close interest in her husband's activities, participated in his plans and their realisation, and also lent a hand herself whenever necessary: a truly astonishing catalogue of achievements for a woman who was just thirty-seven when her husband first fell ill. But life had even more trying challenges in store for her. In the business world, which was at that time almost exclusively a male domain, it was often very difficult for a woman to assert herself and her authority. Marie-Louise put it like this: "I was often given the feeling that I had been called in to meetings in London and Paris just because of the name of Ritz. This state of affairs was understandably difficult to bear. Nonetheless, I was determined to carry on confidently in César's footsteps." As chairman of the board of directors of "The Ritz" hotel in Paris and member of the management committee of the "Ritz Development Company", she also had to review commercial transactions and remain continuously abreast of developments. She received help and encouragement from her two sons, and she had the gift of gathering about her competent employees from the House of Ritz.

Marie-Louise bore her husband two sons: Charles and René. Their younger years coincided with the time when their father was ailing and his condition visibly deteriorating. He who loved his sons with fatherly pride could only watch their education and training from the sidelines, and the responsibility for their care thus lay almost exclusively with their mother. In 1910, when she was presiding over the opening of the hotel "Ritz" in Budapest, in whose construction she had participated, she was informed of a tragic accident involving her younger son, an accident from which he never completely recovered. In March 1918, he succumbed to severe myelitis, and a few months later his father followed him to his grave – a truly tragic year for Marie-Louise.

She carried the burden and responsibility for the hotel company of which her husband had been chairman, and for the management of "The Ritz" in Paris until 1961, when she passed the latter over to her son Charles. The conception, spirit, and tradition of "The Ritz" remained largely intact, although certain concessions had to be made to new trends in the hotel business. "The Ritz" remained "The Ritz", even when no member of the family was active in its

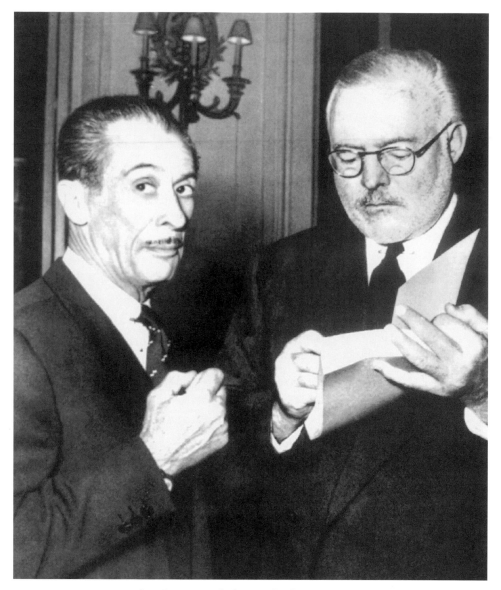

Charles Ritz (left) with the American writer Ernest Hemingway. They were both passionate amateur anglers. In 1954, Charles Ritz published the book "Prise sur le Vif", whose German edition entitled "Erlebtes Fliegen-fischen" ("Experiencing Fly Fishing") was reprinted several times. The foreword was written by Ernest Hemingway, who in the photograph is seen taking a closer look at the original French edition.

management, a function which Monique Ritz, wife of the deceased Charles Ritz, was the last of the family to fulfil.

It was also Marie-Louise who maintained the link with the village of Niederwald, César's home, after her husband's death, and she returned there at regular intervals. She had his parental home renovated and tastefully furnished without disturbing the essential character of the typical mountain farmhouse.

César Ritz and his son René were first buried in the Paris cemetery Père Lachaise. They were later exhumed and taken to rest in the local cemetery in Niederwald. Marie-Louise joined them later.

The fountain which she donated to the parish of Niederwald in 1952 – two years after the 100th anniversary of her husband's birth – unfortunately fell victim to the ravages of time. It has been replaced, however, by a new one which will be a memorial to César Ritz for as long as it flows, and for as long as the modest inscription on his parental house remains.

*Charles and Monique Ritz in the garden of "The Ritz"
in Paris. After the death of Charles Ritz (1976), his wife
Monique took over the management of the hotel.*

FINALE

During his lifetime, César Ritz was hardly noticed or recognised in the canton of Valais or Switzerland in general. There is not one single "Ritz" hotel in the whole country. Was his native land too small for his big plans? Did he foresee that our mountains would never be able to compete with the sophisticated life of the big cities, the expanse and attraction of the ocean, or the comfort of the famous spas which the aristocratic clientele of the hotel "Ritz" demanded? Did the serious, incurable illness wrest the baton from the hand of the great conductor in the concert hall of the international hotel business before he was able realise all his plans? Switzerland and Valais virtually got to know César Ritz only after his death. His name and his personality were, however, mentioned and honoured on the occasion of the Swiss national exhibition in 1939 in Zurich. And a simple but impressive ceremony at which Valais remembered its great son, his life, and his achievements was held in Niederwald in commemoration of the 100th anniversary of his birth.

Long after Ritz's time, the Ritz hotels continued to be regarded as a byword for comfort, elegance, luxury, and peerless examples of service and convenience. In Paris, London, and Madrid they were the scenes and witnesses of important historical events with international repercussions. It is thus not surprising that — especially in the United States of America — the advertising industry latched onto the famous name of Ritz and a launched a wide variety of first-class products under this quality seal. To their credit, however, César Ritz's descendants never seriously sought to make a profit from their world-famous name. But the foundation named after César Ritz will continue to be remembered, because its income makes a considerable contribution towards financing the general and vocational education (study or occupational training) of young people resident in Niederwald. Already a number of the young men and women it has supported have been able to enter professional life with excellent training behind them. They are certain to remember the generous help provided by the Ritz family, which gave them the best possible start in life. How different things were in César's own young days, and for a long time thereafter.

The Ritz Foundation was presided over in succession by Marie-Louise Ritz and Charles Ritz. Its president today is Charles's wife, Monique Ritz.

The burial of César and René Ritz in Niederwald.

THE "CÉSAR RITZ" COLLEGES AND PROGRAMMES

In 1982, Dr. Wolfgang Petri founded the HOTELCON-SULT Swiss Hotel and Catering Colleges in the Hotel Alpina in Brig. The mission of his hotel management training institutes was to combine the Swiss tradition of hospitality and customer service with the rapidly developing management style from the U.S.A. As César Ritz revolutionized the hotel industry at the end of the 19th century, our new concept revolutionized the traditional hotel management educational system in Switzerland.

In 1986, Monique Ritz, wife of Charles Ritz and sole remaining representative of the César Ritz family, gave permission to the Institut Hôtelier, located on the shores of Lake Geneva, to use her father-in-law's name. A few years later the Board of the César Ritz Foundation extended this unique authorization to use the name "César Ritz" for all colleges and programmes managed by HOTELCONSULT, provided they guaranteed the highest academic and professional standards.

The name and mission of César Ritz would thereby inspire future generations of hotel managers around the world.

Today (2005), four "César Ritz" colleges and programmes enroll over 1'000 students from 50 countries at any one time, about half in the Institut Hôtelier "César Ritz" in Le Bouveret and University Centre "César Ritz" in Brig. The "César Ritz" programme at the International College of Hospitality Management in Suffield, U.S.A., has graduated about 2'000 students, and the "César Ritz" programme at the International College of Tourism & Hotel Management in Sydney, Australia, has, since its inauguration in 1996, been successful in educating students in the Asian and Pacific region with the "César Ritz" values. 12'000 graduates from 60 countries proudly carry the values of César Ritz, the most famous hotel pioneer, and we hope that this 'spirit of excellence' will continue in the future, as we are also proud to be an important factor in maintaining the renown of César Ritz.

Our Swiss Diplomas, Bachelor and Master Degrees are recognized worldwide by the hotel industry, and are accredited by educational and professional authorities in the State of Valais, Switzerland, as well as by official accrediting agencies in the U.S.A. and Australia.

"CÉSAR RITZ" COLLEGES AND PROGRAMMES (2005)

Institut Hôtelier "César Ritz",
Le Bouveret, Switzerland

University Centre "César Ritz",
Brig, Switzerland

"César Ritz" Programme at ICHM
Suffield, CT, U.S.A.

"César Ritz" Programme at ICTHM
Sydney, Australia

CHRONOLOGICAL TABLE OF HIS CAREER

1865	Hotel "Couronnes et Poste", Brig: Ritz begins his apprenticeship as a waiter. This apprenticeship, however, is terminated.
1867	Hotel "de la Fidélité", Paris: first, jack-of-all trades and trainee waiter, then assistant waiter.
1868–1869	Paris: Ritz first serves in a bar, in a restaurant with fixed prices, then he learns the job of waiter from the bottom up and works in succession as assistant waiter and waiter.
1869–1871	Restaurant "Le Voisin": Ritz expands and deepens his vocational knowledge and is soon promoted to head waiter. Experiences the occupation of Paris in the Franco-Prussian war.
1872	Waiter and head waiter in the hotel "Splendide" in Paris; first contacts with guests from overseas.
1873	World Exhibition in Vienna, head waiter in the "Les Trois Frères Provençaux" restaurant. Vienna was at this time the meeting place for European aristocracy.
1874	"Grand-Hôtel" in Nice, restaurant manager.
1874	Hotel "Rigi-Kulm": first encounter with Colonel Pfyffer von Altishofen, owner of the hotel "National" in Lucerne.
1875	Head waiter in the "Grand-Hôtel" in Locarno, where the internationally important Locarno Pact was signed in 1923.
1876	San Remo: responsible for service and administration in the hotel "de Nice".
1877	San Remo: director of the "Hôtel Victoria". Here, Ritz takes the initiative in improving the sanitary installations.

1877	Lucerne: director of the hotel "National", which under his management soon experiences a major upswing. Director of the hotel "Les Iles Britanniques" in Menton.
1878–1880	Director of the hotel "Bellevue" in Enghien-les-Bains, lessee of the buffet "Jardins d'Acclimatation" in the Bois de Boulogne, co-owner of the hotel "Les Roches Noires" in La Trouville.
1880–1887	Director of the "Grand-Hôtel" in Monte Carlo and the hotel "National" in Lucerne; meets Auguste Escoffier.
1888–1889	César Ritz becomes the owner of the hotels "de la Conversation" and "Minerva" in Baden-Baden, and of the hotel "de Provence" in Cannes.
1889	Commences management of the hotel "Savoy" in London, which at the time is considered to be exemplary, but from which he breaks away later.
1891–1895	Construction and commissioning of the "Grand-Hôtel" in Rome, which Ritz heads as general director. This hotel is designed to be the *nec plus ultra* of modern living comfort.
1897–1898	Construction and opening of the hotel "Ritz" in Paris.
1898	Opening of the hotel "Carlton" in London.
1890–1900	Additional professional activity as expert and advisor in numerous undertakings in the catering trade.
1902	Illness and thus sudden interruption of his work.